The
Maple Syrup
Book

The Maple Syrup Book

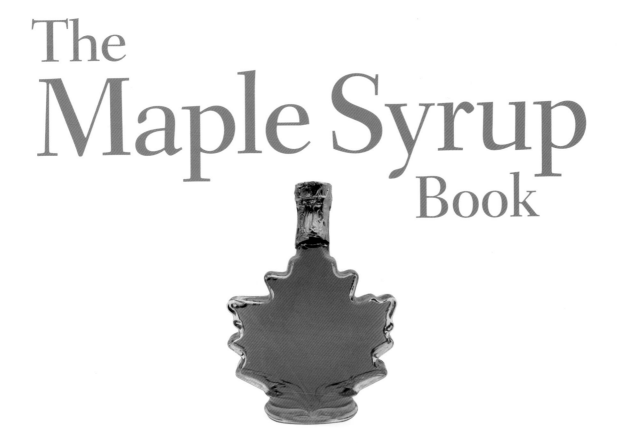

Janet Eagleson & Rosemary Hasner

The BOSTON MILLS PRESS

A Boston Mills Press Book

First printing

In Canada:
Distributed by Firefly Books Ltd.
66 Leek Crescent
Richmond Hill, Ontario, Canada L4B 1H1

In the United States:
Distributed by Firefly Books (U.S.) Inc.
P.O. Box 1338, Ellicott Station
Buffalo, New York 14205

Published by Boston Mills Press, 2006

The Publisher gratefully acknowledges the financial support for our publishing program by the Government of Canada through the Canada Book Fund as administered by the Department of Canadian Heritage.

H

633.6
EAG

4/9/2014

Printed in China.

Library and Archives Canada Cataloguing in Publication

Eagleson, Janet, 1968-
The maple syrup book / Janet Eagleson & Rosemary Hasner.

Includes bibliographical references and index.

ISBN-13: 978-1-77085-033-0 (pbk.)

1. Maple syrup. I. Hasner, Rosemary II. Title.
HD9119.M3E34 2006   664'.132   C2005-906123-5

Publisher Cataloging-in-Publication Data (U.S.)

Eagleson, Janet.
The maple syrup book / Janet Eagleson and Rosemary Hasner.
[96] p. : photos. (chiefly col.) ; cm.

Includes bibliographical resources and index.
Summary: Story behind the North American tradition of maple syrup.

ISBN-13: 978-1-77085-033-0 (pbk.)

1. Maple syrup. I. Hasner, Rosemary. II. Title.
664.132 dc23   HD9119 M3E34 2012

Design by PageWave Graphics Inc.

Contents

Introduction

MY FASCINATION WITH MAPLE SYRUP BEGAN WHEN I WAS TEN YEARS OLD, when my parents moved us into the old farmhouse on the family farm. We had a woodstove for the very first time and there were two maple trees in front of the house that seemed perfect for tapping. Dad helped me and my brother put the taps in. We hung the pails diligently and every day after we hopped off the school bus, we checked for sap. We hounded our mother relentlessly until she let us use her best pot. We filled it with every drop of sap we'd collected — and then we sat beside the woodstove and watched that proverbial pot boil.

When you're ten or eleven, making maple syrup can be a very disheartening experience. We watched all of our sap disappear, leaving only an inch or two of syrup in that pot. But mom used to be a Grade Three teacher, so the experience became a lesson in math, science, social science and geography, an opportunity to help us understand what was happening. A lot of her teachings came back to mind when I started work on this book.

The romance of maple syrup is unmistakable. Sugar shacks, wood fires, sleigh rides, traditional feasts and energetic folk music are woven into the fabric of a northeastern North American springtime.

Next year, I will be able to once again make my own maple syrup — a few of the maple trees outside my country home are finally big enough to tap. I hope you enjoy this book and either try syrup making for yourself or visit a local sugar shack for a little hint of this springtime tradition!

— Janet Eagleson

A History of Maple Syrup

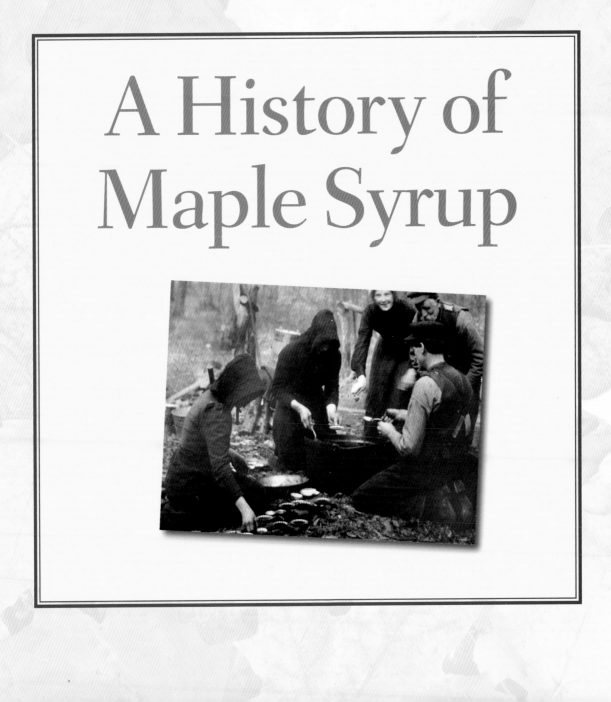

A Gift from the Natives

MAPLE SYRUP WAS FIRST ENJOYED LONG BEFORE NORTH AMERICAN HISTORY recorded its delights in ink or paint or pencil. The origins of this liquid gold come from so far back that the earliest tales of it come from the magic of Native stories, passed down in the oral tradition from generation to generation.

One such story, told in various ways, is the Iroquois legend of Woksis, the great hunter. It is said that one evening in early March, Woksis gently swung his axe into a maple tree before he went to sleep. The next morning, he rose early, removed the axe and left to go on a three-day hunt. While Woksis was away, the maple tree gently "cried" teardrops from the wound left by the axe into a container at the base of the tree. The great hunter's wife found the vessel some three days later and, thinking it was frozen water, used it to prepare a stew for her husband's return.

OPPOSITE: Each North American Native woman in the 1800s and early 1900s would have had up to 1,500 birch bark vessels in use every spring. [Photo circa 1939.]
RIGHT: Hand-sewn containers made from birch bark and stitched with thin fibers of bark or tree root were used to collect sap.

The pot simmered all day long, and soon a sweet aroma filled the air. With each passing hour, the stew tasted better and better. When Woksis finally returned home that evening he devoured the delicious stew, sweetened with the unmistakable flavor of maple, and was so well pleased that he kissed his wife, thus passing on the delightful taste to her as well. From that moment on, the Iroquois gathered the tears of the maple to make their magical sweetener.

Another legend of the people of the Eastern Woodlands tells of the powerful trickster, Nanabush. Nanabush was a mischievous changeling who could take the form of man or animal whenever he wanted. One day, Nanabush arrived in a village of his people only to find it strangely silent. The fires were dead and the gardens were choked with weeds. Worst of all, there was no one there to greet him. The village was completely empty.

They were contented to let it boil a little, to thicken it something, and make a sort of Syrup.

F.W. Waugh, on Iroquois foods and food preparation, 1916

Nanabush knew the people loved the sweet syrup that flowed from the maple trees and so he quickly ran into the woods. There he found every man, woman, child and even dog lying, mouths open and eyes closed, beneath the maple trees, the thick syrup dripping straight into their mouths. His people had given up hunting and fishing and planting, and grown fat and lazy because of the easiness of their lives.

Nanabush decided to change their lazy ways and so, transforming himself into a giant, he scooped up water from the nearby lake and used it to fill the maple trees with water until the syrup became thin and watery. He told his people they could have syrup again, but only when food was scarce, at the end of the winter, when the snow began to melt. And the sap would no longer run thick and sweet, but be thin as water. Only after they gathered the sap and chopped the

Traditionally, Native women ran the sugar-making operations with the help of the children. [Photo circa 1939.]

He willed that there shall be growing forests in which there shall be certain trees from which sap shall habitually fall in its season. So, too, let us give thanks because there still grows here and there maple trees, for we can look upon maple sugar.

Address of Thanksgiving to the Powers of the Master of Life (Green Corn Dance)

wood and built a fire and heated the sweet water from the maples for a very long time would they enjoy the syrup again.

Yet another story says the busy little red squirrel was the first maple sugar maker. Certainly if you go into the woods today you might catch sight of a squirrel nibbling on the tender, thin bark of the maple trees in late winter. The sap drips freely from the spot of the bite and sometimes freezes into a sugar on the branches, offering a tasty snack for all who try it.

Whatever the legend, it is believed Native people both drank the sap of the maple tree and boiled it to make sugar. The Sugar Moon (or Maple Moon to some) — the first full moon of sap season in March or occasionally April — marked the beginning of maple syrup season. The first tapping of the trees was marked by an energetic Maple Dance to give thanks to the Creator for nature's gift, and the Sugar Moon was a joyful celebration of the coming springtime.

The first sugarmakers slashed notches in the trees and gathered the sap in clay or bark containers. They turned the sugary liquid to syrup by dropping rocks heated on a fire into sap held in hollowed-out logs or stone vessels, or by boiling the sap in large pots hanging directly over an open fire. They used this sugar mostly for themselves and occasionally in trade with the early European settlers.

ABOVE: Native North Americans gathered their sap in either clay or birch bark containers.

By the time the Europeans arrived in North America in the middle of the 16th century, the Native people living there had long practised the art of sugaring. It is believed that Native people taught first the French and then the English how to make sugar from the trees. Soon, maple sugar and maple syrup were staples for the settlers, who could not afford to import expensive sugar from the West Indies.

A Family Affair

Family is the most enduring theme in the world of maple syrup. Techniques and tricks are passed down from generation to generation, from parent to child and child again, each one perfecting the methods a little bit more. Regardless of the size of the operation, every available hand is put to work in its production.

This family tradition began with the Native people of northeastern North America. The women were in charge of making the maple sugar, as they were responsible for gathering the food. During the Sugar Moon, the men set down their weapons to help the women gather the sap, and children joined in the work and the celebration. The time was relaxed and joyful.

Pioneer families worked together out of necessity, as their survival depended on it. From an early age, children had a long list of daily tasks they needed to complete and they worked beside their parents whenever they weren't in school. Sugaring time was a time of hard work but, as the family sat and talked while they waited for the sap to become sugar, also a time of bonding, bringing people together in the first warm weeks after a long winter.

Emptying maple sap buckets. [Photo circa 1925.]

Old Order Mennonites near St. Jacobs, Ontario,
sell their finished syrup at local farmers' markets.

Enter the modern era, and the importance of family remains. Many operations have been handed down through the generations, and the insights of parents, grandparents and great-grandparents help today's syrup makers perfect their products. Technological advances such as reverse osmosis reduction, steam- and oil-powered evaporation, tubing, vacuum systems and computerization have made maple syrup production faster, more efficient and less dependent on the work of many hands to get the job done. Still, everyone in the family pitches in where they can, helping with everything from bottling to selling.

Many a stout boy of fourteen or fifteen, with the aid of the mother and young ones, has made sugar enough to supply the family, besides selling a large quantity.

Catherine Parr Traill, *The Canadian Settler's Guide*

Pioneer Sugar Makers

IMAGINE THE HARDSHIPS ENDURED BY THE EARLY SETTLERS TO NORTH America. Arriving at their chosen destination in a strange land, weak and undernourished after a terrifying and dangerous months-long journey across the ocean, they would discover their promise of a new beginning was nothing more than a densely choked tract of forest. Then, with only a few tools and almost no supplies, they had to race against time to clear some land, build a shelter and grow food before the harsh winter arrived.

The complaints of 21st-century multitaskers pale in comparison to those of the hardy souls who settled North America. In order to survive, these pioneers were forced to be self-sufficient. They were builders, butchers, lumberjacks, stonemasons, doctors, weavers, tailors, farmers, blacksmiths and hunters. They relied on the land to provide them with the basics for survival, and soon began to mimic the ways of their

OPPOSITE: Syrup making around the turn of the century was a social affair. Entire families gathered to enjoy good conversation, good fun and, eventually, good food. [Photo circa 1910.] RIGHT: An original 19th-century wooden sap pail.

Native neighbors in harvesting that bounty. Just as the first European settlers in 17th-century Quebec followed the example set by the Native people in hunting, farming and fishing, they also learned how to be sugar makers.

Sugar from the West Indies was as expensive and scarce as gold in the new country. Maple was free and plentiful, and the crop came at a time when the inhabitants could do little else on the land. For several weeks each spring, pioneer families would work from dawn until dusk to fill their cupboards full of maple sugar cakes, more easily stored than syrup, that would last them for the year ahead. Any extra was packed into containers and taken to town to be traded for hardware and other essentials of life. As production methods improved, maple sugar became a commodity itself, to be bought and sold at the local general store.

As settlers began to experiment with different containers and tools, the spile and the bucket came into common use. Augers and drills replaced the axes, and copper or iron kettles became the boiling pots of choice. Later, large racks were built in the woods on which kettles of graduated sizes were hung by chain over separate fires. The sap was carried to the rack by hand or gathered using a horse-drawn sleigh and wooden barrel. The sap was poured into the largest kettle and boiled over a fast fire. When the sap reduced and got darker, it was transferred to the next smaller pot, where it was boiled some more. The liquid got even darker in this pot and was then poured into

ABOVE: Early Canadians like the Henderson family of Millbank, Ontario, collected sap by hand. OPPOSITE: In the 19th century, kettles of graduated sizes were hung by chain over open fires to produce maple syrup.

Hour after hour,
all through the day and
most of the night,
the fire under the pots
was kept blazing.

Hour after hour
all day long,
the patient horses
drew a jumper sleigh
and a barrel down the
bush trails from tree
to tree collecting sap
from the brimming pails.

Hour after hour
we fed the kettles,
pouring in sap and still
more sap as the boiling
diminished that which
was already in pots.

Kenneth McNeill Wells, *The Owl Pen*

Pioneer syrup making is reenacted at festivals such as this one at Bruce's Mill Conservation Area near Stouffville, Ontario.

the smallest pot, where it was finished into maple sugar. A small shelter or shanty built near the boiling place helped protect the settlers from the elements while they worked. It not only acted as a windbreak but also as a storage place for the wood needed to keep the fires roaring.

By the mid- to late 19th century, some sugar makers began experimenting with a more complex system. They used sheet metal to make shallow, flat-bottomed pans in which they made their syrup, and they began to try out different metal spouts, pails and lids.

Soon, the flat-bottomed pans gave way to the first evaporators, which featured multiple compartments and channels through which the sap and syrup flowed, and even featured ridges on the bottom of the pans, an invention that increased the surface area that could be heated and dramatically reduced the time required to turn sap into syrup and sugar.

Next came the arch, which suspended the pans above the fire without support from above and allowed the fire to be lit in a box underneath. The fire could be adjusted so certain areas burned hotter and faster than others, and the smoke produced was vented out a chimney at the back. These evaporators moved indoors into buildings especially constructed for them, making the production of maple syrup cleaner and more controlled than ever before.

From tapping the trees by hand to waiting for the syrup to boil over an open fire, sugaring off was a slow process for the pioneers.

This basic evaporator design has not really changed since the late 1900s. It was just before the turn of the 20th century that maple syrup became a more precious commodity than maple sugar, and soon it was to become the liquid gold of Canada and the American northeast.

Making Maple Syrup

Rarer than Gold

MAPLE SYRUP CAN BE MADE ONLY IN A RELATIVELY SMALL GEOGRAPHIC area in northeastern North America — other parts of the world either don't have the right temperatures or the right trees to make this delicious stuff!

Thomas Jefferson transplanted young maples from Vermont to his plantation at Monticello, in Virginia, but because the more southern location lacked the right combination of freezing nights and warm days, the trees survived but failed to produce any syrup.

The province of Quebec is by far the single-largest maple syrup producer in the world. In 2006, Quebec boasted between 7,000 and 8,000 syrup makers who made close to 10.8 million U.S. gallons (almost 41 million liters) of maple syrup. That's about 75 percent of the world's volume of maple syrup!

The province also boasts some of the largest maple syrup operations in the world, with over 140 operators running at least 30,000 taps every year. Some operators even boast more than 100,000 taps! Their neighbors in Ontario average close to 600 taps per

OPPOSITE: Some Quebec syrup makers make sugaring-off parties an all-inclusive destination, complete with accommodations right in the sugar bush, hearty breakfasts, music and more. This cabin is at Sucrerie de la Montagne, near Rigaud, Quebec.

I have never seen a reason why every farmer should not have a sugar orchard, as well as an apple orchard. The supply of sugar for his family would require as little ground, and the process of making it as easy as cider.

Thomas Jefferson, Letter to M. Lasteyrie, July 1808

operation with a mere handful of them running with 7,500 taps or more!

Vermont, which is the second largest syrup producer in the world, saw significant fluctuations in syrup volumes in the last decade. In 2003, Vermont produced 358,500 U.S. gallons. That rose to 460,000 in 2006 and a whopping 1,140,000 in 2011. That's the highest yield on Vermont record in the last 60 years!

New Brunswick, Ontario, Maine and New York are next largest on the list but production doesn't stop there. There are successful maple farmers in Wisconsin, Pennsylvania, Ohio, Michigan, New Hampshire, Massachusetts, Nova Scotia and Connecticut.

So, what happens to all of that syrup? Not surprisingly, much of it is exported to other parts of the world where maple syrup cannot be made. In 2006, Canada exported over $190 million of maple syrup to 45 countries, including the United States, European and Asian nations. Maple syrup is big business!

ABOVE: Dick O'Brien of Uncle Richard's Maple Syrup and Supplies near Mount Forest, Ontario, shows off the fruit of his labor. LEFT: There's a right size bottle for everyone. OPPOSITE: Experienced syrup makers know the color of perfect maple syrup. Here, Pierre Faucher of Sucrerie de la Montagne near Rigaud, Quebec, checks the color of his delicious liquid gold.

29

Quebec

"Sugaring off" is an extraordinary springtime tradition in Quebec. The experience is just like an old-time community party, where everyone is friendly and no one ever feels left out. Imagine feasts of back bacon, baked beans, pea soup, home-made bread, tourtière, country sausages, eggs, sugar pie and more, and partygoers leaping up from long, food-laden tables to sing and dance with perfect strangers sitting at the next table! Food drizzled with maple syrup is passed freely, a large open fireplace crackles with light and heat, and the sounds of fiddles, spoons and clogs fill the air of the *cabane à sucre* — the sugar shack.

Sugaring-off parties in Quebec combine food, music and friendship. Nelson Carter of Montreal, Quebec, fiddles, sings and entertains at a traditional Quebecois celebration.

The smells, sounds and sights of sugaring off in Quebec conjure up a more romantic time of years past, when families and communities came together over song, dance and food to celebrate the arrival of spring. One such event takes place every year at Sucrerie de la Montagne in Rigaud, Quebec, about 45 minutes west of Montreal.

From the moment they arrive, visitors will feel as if they have stepped back into another era. The sugar shack's owner, Pierre Faucher, looks just like what you might have imagined when reading about the voyageurs in your elementary school history text. The room itself — a historic log barn painstakingly restored to its pioneer glory — is warm and comfortable, just like grandmother's kitchen. And the serving staff wears traditional Quebecois dress, complete with colorful woven sashes.

Nothing can prepare you for the pure joy of a traditional, Quebecois sugaring-off party. If you've never been to a *cabane à sucre* in springtime, take the opportunity. You'll never experience anything quite like it.

The tables are set and the party is set to begin every spring in Quebec.

Vermont

One word comes to mind when describing Vermont syrupmakers — precision. Technological innovation drives many of Vermont's operators in their quest for perfect maple syrup. They are constantly working on ways to improve their efficiency and reduce their costs while boiling better and better maple syrup. A recent innovation — the microspout — was developed in northern Vermont to help reduce stress on the trees.

Vermont's 2,500 or so maple syrup producers work within some of the tightest production and food inspection regulations in the world. Government agents make surprise inspections throughout the year to check for proper grading and syrup

In Vermont, several producers have switched to the microspout, a home-grown innovation that reduces damage to trees when tapped and may help sustain the lives of centuries-old maples such as this beauty.

density. They spend most of their time educating operators on how to achieve the proper grade for their product rather than issuing tickets for violations, but operators do face fines of up to $1,000 for improperly labeled syrup.

Vermont syrup makers work in relative peace and quiet during springtime syrup season. There are only a handful of in-season festivals and drop-ins to the sugar shacks are rare. The busiest time for Vermont producers is autumn, when the leaves turn color and the undulating countryside presents a vivid kaleidoscope of crimson, copper, russet and ochre. The views draw leaf-peeping locals and tourists like a magnet!

Vermont maple syrup has a slightly higher sugar density than other maple syrups. Try some for yourself and see if you can taste the difference!

RIGHT: The Vermont Maple Outlet is owned and operated by the Marsh family, whose ancestors have been producing syrup since 1793. Today, they produce about 3,000 gallons of syrup from 7,200 taps, 9 miles of main lines and 40 miles of lateral lines. ABOVE: The maple syrup shingle hangs from many a barn and sugar shacks across the state.

Ontario

Ontario is home to a wide range of maple syrup producers and festivals, including the world's largest single-day maple syrup festival, which is held in Elmira every year. Visitors to the event, which draws more than 60,000 people, pack the main street shopping for syrup products, tasting samples and enjoying the festivities.

Elmira, Ontario, hosts the world's largest single-day maple syrup festival every year.

Elmira is located in Waterloo, the largest syrup-producing district in Ontario. (Lanark County near Ottawa, which hails itself Ontario's Maple Capital, is the second-largest producing area in the province.)

One of the most unique maple syrup sights in the province can be found in the Waterloo region. The area is home to thousands of Mennonites, including many Old Order Mennonites who dress in traditional dark garb, straw hats and bonnets, and drive horse-drawn buggies. These quiet people forego most of the amenities we take for granted — electricity, television and cars — to live simply off the land, protected from the outside world by the supports of a tightly bound community. Many of them still make maple syrup the old-fashioned way, using buckets instead of tubing and pipelines, and sell their finished products at local farmers' markets, from their kitchens or at the ends of their driveways.

The rest of the lower half of the province is dappled with small- to medium-sized family-run operations. Ontario operators focus on production yet still open the doors of their sugar shacks to passers-by who

Many of the Old Order Mennonites in Waterloo County sell their syrup at the end of their driveways.

are interested in discovering the magic of maple. Several operators work to replicate the old-fashioned feel of Quebec's sugaring-off parties with pancake feasts, horse-drawn sugar bush tours and fiddle music.

Some Ontario syrup makers participate in a unique quality-assurance program called "The Ontario Maple Seal of Quality," opening their doors every three years to government inspectors who focus first on the quality of the syrup and then turn their eyes to the entire operation, from tree and woodlot management right through the bottling process.

Which Maple Is Which?

North America boasts thirteen native maple species, but only two — sugar and black — are the preferred trees for maple syrup production. Two others — red and silver — are sometimes tapped by backyard or roadside hobbyists, but they are not frequently used in large operations.

Sugar Maple

The sugar maple grows throughout most of southeastern Canada and northeastern United States. Its bright green, distinctively notched leaves have five lobes with smooth edges. (No tiny "teeth" appear along the edges of the leaves.) The leaves are 3 to 5 inches (8 to 15 cm) from edge to edge, and they emerge directly opposite each other along the small branches of the tree. The bark of the sugar maple is smooth and gray on smaller trees, but becomes furrowed with deep ridges as the tree grows. It takes anywhere between forty to sixty years for sugar maples to grow to a size suitable for tapping, and the trees can live several hundreds of years.

The black maple is so similar to the sugar maple it is often mistaken for its cousin. The bark and leaves are only slightly darker than the sugar's, and the leaves are more likely to have three large lobes instead of five. The black maple has a much narrower range than the sugar maple, growing mostly in the north central part of the United States and in the southernmost edge of southern Ontario. It is not commonly found in the areas of highest maple syrup production — Quebec, parts of Ontario and Vermont.

Sugar maple leaves usually have five lobes with smooth edges.

Red Maple

The red maple is one of the most widespread maple species in North America. It is found everywhere from Newfoundland west to Manitoba in Canada, and across the eastern half of the United States. Its light green, sharply notched leaves almost always have three lobes (sometimes five) with tiny, sharp teeth along the edges. The leaves vary in width from 2 to 6 inches (5 to 15 cm). The bark of young red maples is similar to that of sugar maples (smooth and gray), but becomes dark brown and scaly as the tree matures.

LEFT: Red maple leaves are light green with tiny, sharp teeth along the edges. RIGHT: The silver maple's deeply notched lobes make it easy to identify.

Silver Maple

The silver maple is a fast-growing shade tree that is found in the southern parts of Ontario and Quebec in Canada, and throughout most of the eastern United States. Its large 5-to-7-inch (15 to 20 cm), deeply notched leaves have a distinct silvery-white underside and tiny teeth along the outside edges. The bark on young trees is smooth and gray, but quickly grows scaly, leaving long, thin plates of shaggy-looking bark that curve outward from the tree's trunk.

All four of these maples produce delicious syrup, but it is the sugar and black maples that are the preferred trees for the commercial production of maple syrup. It's really a matter of convenience and economics.

The sap of red and silver maples contains less sugar, which means it takes more sap, more time and a lot more money to produce syrup with it. Red and silver maples are ready to tap earlier than sugar and black maples. The deeper snow on the ground at this time makes it much harder for the syrup maker to get through the forest to collect the sap. Also, red and silver maples bud very quickly, which makes the opportunity for tapping very short. (You can't make syrup once the tree buds.) And finally, the boiling of red and silver maple sap leaves behind a lot more "sugar sand" — the concentrated minerals that are left behind in the evaporator — after boiling. This substance is harmless but it tends to clog the machinery and means time-consuming and frequent cleaning of the evaporator is necessary.

How Maple Syrup Is Made

THE WAY MAPLE SAP FLOWS INSIDE TREES IS ONE OF THE LEAST UNDERSTOOD mysteries in nature. The "sap-flow mechanism" — the movement of sap up and down the tree from the roots to the stems and back — is so complex, even scientists have had trouble defining and understanding the process.

Maple sap is the watery, slightly sweet fluid produced by the cells of maple trees. It is mostly water, with a sugar content of somewhere between two and three percent. It also includes amino acids, phenolic compounds, organic acids and traces of vitamins and minerals including potassium and calcium. These are stored in the tree during its growing season from May to September. Very simply, sap is the food that feeds the tree's roots, trunk, branches and leaves.

OPPOSITE: On a good day, the sap from this tap might drip close to 60 times every minute.
RIGHT: Maple trees produce delicious syrup in springtime and gorgeous colors in fall.

Think of a maple tree, but picture in your mind a round container with skinny drinking straws lining the outer edge. Look down at the container from the top — this is the easiest way to imagine what the inside of a maple tree looks like.

The sap moves up and down those straws, moving from the roots to the leaves and back. This thin, outside edge of the tree is called sapwood.

How does sap move inside the trees? Carbon dioxide gas builds up inside maple trees during winter and in the freezing temperatures of spring nights. As the trees warm up on sunny spring days, the pressurized gas forces the sap to move. When a hole is drilled into a tree's sapwood, it's just like poking a hole into one of those straws — some of the tree's sap will immediately start to trickle out the hole. This occurs because the pressure inside the tree is greater than it is outside. Now insert a tap, hang a bucket, and sap collection can begin!

Tapping will never harm the tree as long as the tree is healthy and the number of taps is limited to the quantity recommended. (See Number of Taps on page 45.)

The sap will run anytime when temperatures move above and below freezing (usually in February and March). Warm days, around 36°F to 47°F (2°C to 7°C) and cool nights, around 25°F to 21°F (-4°C to -6°C), will produce the most sap. Sap stops flowing when the temperature stays above or below freezing for long periods, but will start again when the proper temperature cycle (warm and cool) happens again. Sap stops entirely when these temperature cycles end for the season. The total length of the season is only four to six weeks.

Never yet
*   was a springtime,*
Late though
*   lingered the snow,*
That the sap
*   stirred not*
*   at the whisper*
Of the southwind,
*   sweet and low...*

Margaret Elizabeth Sangster

Tapping and Collecting

Much of the romance of traditional maple syrup production has been lost in the 21st century. Only backyard and roadside hobbyists and Mennonites still continue to use galvanized buckets or plastic pails and spouts. Large commercial operations with hundreds or thousands of taps now rely on plastic tubing, pipelines and, in many cases, vacuum pumps.

However, tapping methods have remained the same for centuries; only the tools of the trade have changed. A few purists, mostly those with only a few taps, may choose to drill tap holes using a hand brace. When hundreds or thousands of holes must be drilled, many producers now use specialized, gasoline-powered tappers.

The trees can be tapped when the temperature rises to near the freezing point, usually late February or early March, depending on the year and the geographic location. Tapping into frozen bark and wood can split the tree, leaving a large and permanent scar. Producers using sealed tubing and a pipeline system can tap earlier than those using buckets, but they need to exercise great caution to ensure no damage to the trees occurs. The smaller, $\frac{5}{16}$-inch "health" spiles are used on the pipeline system to help limit damage to the trees.

Holes are drilled on an upward angle to a depth of no more than 3 inches (7.5 cm). If the wood shavings turn

ABOVE: Man tapping a maple tree for sap, circa 1925. ABOVE LEFT: Assorted spiles from the late 19th and early 20th centuries.

brown or gold, the holes are too deep or the drill has hit a "bad spot." Smart tappers always tap at least 6 inches (15 cm) to either side and slightly above the previous year's tap hole. Remarkably, the tree grows right around these scars as it continues to get larger.

Tapping is part science and part luck. Tap late and you risk missing the precious early runs that often produce the lightest and most valuable syrup. Tap early and you risk low production. The perfect time to tap boils down to an educated guess, past experience and observation of others.

LEFT: Sap pails in the early 20th century were made with whatever materials were available at the time. RIGHT: Today, timesaving, gravity-fed plastic tubing and pipeline have all but replaced traditional buckets.

Number of Taps

The Ontario Tapping Rule is one guide to help you determine the number of taps you can safely put on your tree without damaging it. Remember, the tree diameter must be measured at about chest height (4 feet, 6 inches, or 1.4 m).

Tree diameter	Number of taps
Under 10 inches (25 cm)	0
10 to 14 inches (25 to 35 cm)	1
15 to 19 inches (38 to 49 cm)	2
20 to 24 inches (50 to 60 cm)	3*
over 25 inches (63-plus cm)	4*

* Some syrup makers have embraced the more conservative practice of putting a maximum of two taps in even their largest trees. Backyard syrup makers would be wise to follow this cautious approach with their shade trees regardless of the tree's size to help protect against unnecessary stress and damage. After all, the trees in your yard are there to provide beauty and shade first, and syrup second. The tree must be at least 10 inches (25 cm) in diameter before you can safely tap it.

LEFT: Look closely — this cross-section of a sugar maple shows all of the old (healed) spile holes from years past. RIGHT: The diameter of the tree determines the number of taps it can support.

Sap bucket covers keep snow, rain, sticks and fingers out of the sap.

Sap collected in buckets must be gathered at least once a day because it spoils quickly. Small operators with only a few trees can transfer the sap into a large pail and carry it to the evaporator by hand...if they're particularly strong or a little crazy. A full bucket of sap weighs more than 30 pounds (13 kg) so transferring it to a tank on a sleigh or wagon, depending on the terrain, saves both time and back pain. At the sugar shack, the mobile tank is emptied into the main storage tank, which feeds into the evaporator.

Timesaving, gravity-fed plastic tubing and pipeline have all but replaced buckets in large operations. Plastic spiles are inserted into the tap holes and small plastic tubes are attached to the outside tips of the spiles. These small tubes drop down to a lateral line which can support sap flow from up to 25 taps

The Maple Syrup Museum of Ontario in St. Jacob's, Ontario, is a great place to learn about Native, pioneer and modern syrup-making methods.

depending on the ground's slope. The lateral lines lead to a main line that travels through the sugarbush to a holding tank. Several main lines will fork through the forest toward the holding tank in an intricate web of tubes. Sap from the holding tank is then pumped to the elevated main storage tank located beside the evaporator at the sugar shack.

Plastic lines move sap through the force of gravity or vacuum. Gravity systems rely on the slope of the forest floor to naturally transport the sap from the higher-sitting trees to the lower-lying tank. Vacuum pumps do not suck sap from the trees but rather help artificially lower the pressure in the pipeline system to allow the sap to flow more freely out the spiles (because sap runs best when the pressure inside the tree is higher than outside). Vacuum systems only work when the tubing systems are properly designed and have no air leaks. Unlike tapping, the collection of sap through tubing systems is all science. You'll be frustrated if you rely solely on luck.

ABOVE: John Williams of Pine Farm near Hillsdale, Ontario, checks to see how much sap is in his holding tank. RIGHT: Gravity-fed sap ladders help move sap toward holding tanks in the sugar bush.

48

Organic Certification

Environmental responsibility and "organics" have become key buzzwords of the 21st century. More and more, people are demanding products that are grown or produced in a manner that puts the least amount of stress possible on the world around them. While most syrup producers tend to describe their product as "organic," there are certain, very strict regulations operators need to follow to be able to label their product as "Certified, organic maple syrup."

Producers in Canada must use either stainless steel buckets or plastic tubing to collect their maple sap, and they must never use high vacuum pressure or foreign substances to improve sap flow from the trees. The use of fertilizers, sprays or pesticides on maple trees is strictly forbidden, and cattle cannot pasture or graze in the woodlot. Strict restrictions limit the size of tree tapped and the number of spouts in each tree. Special, phosphorous- and acid-free cleaning solutions must be used in the operation and each producer must have a plan to ensure the long-term health of their trees.

Demand for certified organic maple syrup, which commands an even higher selling price than "regular" maple syrup, is growing.

Successful syrup makers put on a good show, including Bob Finney of Bob's Sugar Shack in Caledon East, Ontario.

Ken and Rene McCutcheon of McCutcheon's Sugar Shack of Coldwater, Ontario, use the power of steam to produce their maple syrup.

Evaporation

The magical process by which the clear, slightly sweet sap turns to liquid gold is . . . boiling it. And boiling it. And then boiling it some more. It takes an astonishing 40 pails of sap to make one pail of maple syrup. Maple sap contains almost 97 percent water, but maple syrup contains no more than about 33 percent water. The "white smoke" you see billowing up from sugar shacks in February and March is actually steam rising up through special "smokestacks" or vents through the roof as the sap is boiled.

Boiling syrup is best done outdoors or in a sugar shack because of the amount of steam produced. Those with only a handful of taps can safely make syrup indoors in a pot on their woodstove or stovetop. Some small operators boil sap in a simple, stainless steel pan over an open fire, camp stove or old gas range.

Syrup makers with a large number of taps use flue-type evaporators to make their liquid gold. These evaporators have a contained firebox to produce heat, and multiple pans that allow the sap to flow continuously through on its way from watery sap to sugary syrup. Some evaporators even have a built-in sap preheater to improve boiling efficiency (adding ice-cold sap to the evaporator has the same slowing effect as adding cold water to a pot of boiling water on your stove).

The sap pan at the back of the evaporator often has flues or deep channels to provide more surface area for heating the sap. A float controls the volume of sap in this pan, keeping it at a certain level, and a pipe connects the sap pan to the syrup pan at the front of the evaporator. The syrup

Syrup produces a lot more steam than a hot shower!

51

How poor are they that have not patience!

William Shakespeare, "Othello"

pans have connected channels that allow the syrup to move across the pans from one side to the other as it becomes sweeter. The firebox or heat source is usually located under the syrup pans.

When the syrup reaches the final channel and its sugar concentration is almost perfect, it is usually "drawn off" for finishing on another, more controllable heat source. Only old-time veteran syrup makers take up the challenge to finish their syrup to the perfect sugar density in their large evaporators. The risk of scalding or burning syrup is so great it takes a steady hand and incredible concentration to achieve perfection on an evaporator.

Evaporators come in various sizes — from the size of a bathtub to almost as big as a small room — and with a wide range of heat sources. Larger evaporators are more efficient because they remove water faster. Wood-fired evaporators are the most common units in use today, followed by those fueled with oil. Natural gas and propane are sometimes used as fuel sources,

ABOVE: Visualize a maze and you'll have a good idea of what these flues and channels look like. OPPOSITE: Pierre Faucher of the award-winning Sucrerie de la Montagne in Rigaud, Quebec, tends the fire in his evaporator.

and propane is a popular choice for finishing syrup in a separate pan. A few syrup makers use steam to make their syrup. While steam systems are expensive to install and require a high level of technical knowledge to operate, they are much faster and more efficient than both wood and oil.

Reverse osmosis is sometimes used in large maple syrup operations to reduce boiling time and increase overall efficiency. This system removes anywhere from

50 to 75 percent of the water from raw sap and creates a concentrate that is then boiled into syrup. The concentrate becomes syrup in a shorter time than sap does, saving the operator money on fuel and helping reduce environmental impact.

Regardless of the type of evaporator and fuel used, the characteristic flavor and color of maple syrup is developed through the evaporation process. Each producer will tell you their syrup and methods are the best. Try as many as you can and decide for yourself!

The evaporator is at the center of every operation.

Finishing and Filtering

Sap becomes syrup at approximately 7°F (4°C) above the boiling point of water. It may sound simple, but it is anything but. The boiling point of water changes every single day and sometimes even during the same day (which is why cookies sometimes bake faster or slower than they did the last time you made them).

The legal sugar density for commercial maple syrup makers ranges from 66.0 to 67.0 percent in Canada and from 66.9 to 68.9 percent in Vermont. In Canada, producers often aim for syrup that is somewhere between 66.6 and 66.9 percent sugar; in Vermont, producers often use 67.0 percent as a benchmark.

To achieve a 66.7-percent sugar density, syrup makers must first measure the boiling point of water, add 7.38°F (4.1°C), and then heat the syrup to this temperature. This process is so sensitive that syrup makers must either measure the boiling point of water on a continuous basis (using a computer-controlled device) or periodically throughout the boiling day.

If the temperature changes just a single degree, the sugar density of the finished syrup will range anywhere from 64 percent (spoils easily) to 69 percent (crystals may form). In either case, the syrup's quality will be dramatically affected. Precision is critical in syrup making.

Some adventurous syrup makers finish their syrup right in the evaporator. Most syrup makers are mere mortals and finish their syrup in a separate finishing pan over which they have much greater control to prevent overheating, scalding, burning and a whole host of potential problems.

An automatic draw-off opens when the temperature of the syrup in the evaporator reaches a set point to prevent the syrup from scalding or burning. The near-perfect syrup is then transferred to a finishing pan to reach the perfect sugar density.

When the syrup reaches the set sugar density, a draw-off valve on the evaporator automatically opens and the near-perfect syrup pours into a container for finishing.

The finishing pan is usually some kind of large, stainless-steel box with a lid, handles, a built-in thermometer and a draw-off spigot or valve.

Syrup makers use a hydrometer, which looks a lot like a thermometer with a chubby bottom, to check sugar density while finishing. Syrup is poured into a tall cup and the hydrometer is placed in the syrup, beside an actual thermometer. The hydrometer floats in the syrup, leaving the measuring tip above the edge of the cup. Syrup producers simply read the level on the hydrometer stem at the top of the cup to calibrate their system to determine the proper sugar density.

Finished maple syrup must still be filtered to remove "sugar sand" before it can be put into containers. Sugar sand is very simply the concentrate of some of the organic acids and minerals found in maple sap. They are harmless but leave syrup with a gritty texture if not removed. Once the syrup is either poured or forced through a series of filters to remove the sugar sand, it is ready for grading.

ABOVE: Adam Leek and family of Leek Farms near Alliston, Ontario, have been making syrup since 1994. ABOVE RIGHT: Antique thermometers. RIGHT: John Williams of Pine House Farm in Hillsdale, Ontario, uses a hydrometer to check the sugar density of his syrup.

Finished syrup is poured through a filter before bottling.

Decorative glass syrup containers allow the beautiful golden hues of the syrup to shine through.

Grading and Packaging

Syrup meant to be sold is graded by color using a measure of the amount of light that passes through it. The lighter the syrup, the more light that passes through, the higher the grade. The grade must be clearly labeled on every package of syrup regardless of where it was produced. The grade given depends on the province or state where it is produced, so it can be a bit confusing. See Which Grade Is Best? on page 75.

Stop in for a sample at Jacques and Pauline Couture's sugar shack near Westfield, Vermont.

Maple syrup is packed into bottles, tins and jugs while it is hot (at least 180°F/82°C) to eliminate potential sources of contamination. Once filled and capped, each container is laid on its side or inverted to sterilize the inside of the cap.

There seem to be as many different ways to pack maple syrup as there are grades of syrup. Metal tins hearken back to a simpler time and are often used for the larger volume packages. Glass bottles allow the beautiful golden hues of the syrup to be seen. They are often used for sizes up to about a quart, or one liter. Coated plastic containers are an excellent alternative to metal for large volumes (up to about a gallon, or 4 liters).

Some large industrial syrup producers hot pack their syrup into large drums for bulk storage. These drums are kept in climate-controlled comfort until they are sold as drums, or reheated for packaging into the smaller containers purchased for use at home.

Make Your Own Maple Syrup

Anyone who has tried to make maple syrup in their backyard has probably suffered through their share of embarrassments and mistakes. But at the end of the day, homemade maple syrup, no matter how dark it is or how many errors were made along the way, is still a thousand times better than any of those imitation maple syrups from grocery store shelves. The most remarkable part of syrup making is the pure satisfaction and pride of making something with your own hands. It's easy to get started. Most of the things you'll need can be found around the house or at the local farm supply or hardware store.

There is no great achievement that is not the result of patient working and waiting.

J. G. Holland

Supplies you'll need

- Hand or power drill with a 7/16-inch (1.1 cm) drill bit
- Spiles with hooks (to hang your buckets)
- Hammer or mallet
- Sap buckets with lids (both must be food grade)
- Large plastic pail
- Large pot or pan
- Cheesecloth, felt or cone-shaped paper coffee filters
- Canning jars or bottles
- Cooking or candy thermometer that extends several degrees beyond the boiling point of water
- Oven mitts, slotted spoons and a sieve

Clean Your Equipment

Start by cleaning all of your equipment with a solution of one part unscented bleach and 20 parts water. Be sure to rinse everything well with hot water and let it dry completely. (It's a good idea to clean and sterilize your equipment at the end of the season too.)

Pick Your Tree

Select a maple tree (see Which Maple is Which? on page 36) that is at least 10 inches (25 cm) in diameter at chest height (4.5 feet high — about 1.5 m). Never tap a tree that is smaller than this size — you will do permanent damage to the tree!

Tap Your Tree

Drill a hole at about chest height on the sunny (south) side of the tree. Drill on an upward angle into the white-colored inner wood to a depth of no more than 3 inches (7.5 cm). This will help protect the inner wood from disease and insects.

If your tree is more than 18 inches (45 cm) in diameter, you can drill a second hole. It should be at least 6 inches (15 cm) away from the first hole (measured horizontally). You can drill the hole slightly higher or lower than the first to keep the buckets and lids from hitting each other.

Never drill the holes when the temperature is below 25°F (-3.8°C) — the tree will still be frozen and you'll rip the wood, causing permanent damage. Gently tap the spiles into the holes with the hook pointing down. If it's a sunny day, the sap may start to flow down the spout right away!

Collect the Sap

Hang your bucket on the hook just below the spile. Attach a cover to the pail to prevent rain, bugs and bark from dropping into the sap.

Collect your sap at least once a day. If you leave it longer than a day, the sap may spoil or freeze overnight (splitting your bucket). Store sap in your freezer if you cannot boil it right away or if you only collect a small amount each day. Before boiling or storing, strain your sap through a piece of cotton fabric (a pillowcase works well) to remove any foreign objects or debris.

Boil the Sap

This is where your patience will be tested. For every 40 pails of sap you collect, you'll be rewarded with one pail of syrup. Maple sap has only about 3 percent sugar in it, so it takes a lot to produce that delicious, golden syrup.

As children, my brother and I "borrowed" our mother's best cooking pot and made our syrup on a wood stove. This stove-top method worked well for the two buckets we hung in front of the house. Boiling indoors creates a lot of steam, so it's best to move outdoors if you tap more than one or two trees.

Fill your pot with sap and bring it to a boil. Many people insist a wood fire is the only way to make maple syrup. Propane-powered corn roasters or barbecues also work well, particularly in places where an open fire is impractical or illegal.

As the sap boils, it starts to turn a wonderful amber-gold color and a distinctive maple aroma will fill the air. You may find that a foam forms on top of the liquid — this is natural. Use your slotted spoon or sieve to remove it and continue boiling.

Always keep about one inch (2.5 cm) of liquid in your pot. If the level goes below this point, you risk scorching or burning your syrup, and all of your patience and hard work to this point will be lost! If you're concerned about burning your syrup, remove it from the heat source and take it inside to your stove to "finish" it.

Your syrup is done when it has a sugar content of 66 to 67 percent (66.7 is optimal).

How can you find out your syrup's sugar content? It may sound complicated, but it isn't. Gently boil some water on your stove and insert your cooking thermometer into the pot. Everyone knows water boils at 212°F (100°C), but many people don't know the barometric pressure will change that boiling point by a little bit every single day! Once you learn the boiling point of water on the day you're making syrup, you can use that same thermometer to check the temperature of your syrup. Syrup that is 66 percent sugar will boil at just under

40°F (4°C) above the boiling point of water. Simply add 40°F (4°C) to the number you calculated from the boiling water and wait for your golden treasure to bubble.

Filter and Bottle

You can use any jar or bottle for your syrup as long as it's clean and has been thoroughly rinsed. Filter your syrup through felt, cheesecloth or a couple of cone-shaped coffee filters stacked together to remove the sugar sand (a natural and harmless by-product of boiling). Pour the filtered syrup into the bottle, attach the cap, and then place the container on its side to sterilize the lid.

Sugar on Snow and Other Delights

PURE MAPLE SYRUP CAN BE TRANSFORMED INTO SEVERAL OTHER DELIGHTFUL maple products, including maple sugar, maple cream or butter and molded maple candies. All are deliciously sweet and are rarely used in large quantities.

Granulated maple sugar is made by heating maple syrup to a temperature 45°F to 50°F (25°C to 27°C) above the boiling point of water. It is then stirred (and stirred and stirred) until it turns into tiny granules, much like the raw sugar you sometimes see in fancy coffee shops. Stirring takes time and muscle power, so a heavy-duty mechanical mixer is often used to save the sugar maker's arms from tiring.

Maple cream or butter is made by heating syrup to a temperature 22°F to 24°F (12°C to 13°C) above the boiling point of water. Once this temperature is reached, the syrup is immediately removed from the heat source and cooled rapidly in a shallow pan. When the syrup is cooled to approximately 50°F (10°C) or lower, it is returned to room

OPPOSITE: Sugar on snow — maple taffy — is a popular item at the Elmira Maple Syrup Festival. RIGHT: For a sweet start to your day, try a little maple butter on toast.

65

Maple lollipops are a favorite of young and old, and they just seem to last forever!

temperature and stirred until it loses its shiny appearance. Then the spread is transferred to small containers and is ready for sale.

Maple candies — by far the most popular product made from maple syrup — are extremely sweet with a concentrated maple flavor. They are made by boiling maple syrup to a temperature 32°F to 34°F (18°C to 19°C) above the boiling point of water. The pans of cooked syrup are then allowed to cool to at least 200°F (93°C) but no cooler than 160°F (71°C), stirred and then packed or poured into rubber molds of different shapes.

Of course, maple taffy, or "sugar on snow" is probably one of the most anticipated and memorable parts of maple syrup season. Maple syrup is heated to

ABOVE: Deliciously sweet maple candies are made in special molds. LEFT: Antique hand-carved sugar molds.

a temperature 35°F to 40°F (19°C to just over 22°C) above the boiling point of water and is then immediately poured, without stirring, onto snow or ice. Wait a few seconds and then either peel the gooey taffy from the snow with your fingers or twirl it onto a stick and enjoy!

Enjoying
Maple Syrup

A Many-Flavored Thing

CAN YOU DESCRIBE THE TASTE OF MAPLE SYRUP? AFTER "MAPLE," MOST SYRUP lovers are at a loss to describe the taste of their favorite grade of syrup.

Syrup has long been described by its color — extra light (fancy), light, medium, amber and dark — with virtually no universal words to describe its taste. The best any of us could do is say we liked, or disliked, the flavor.

Then, a significant taste breakthrough occurred early in 2004 — Agriculture and Agri-Food Canada/Centre Acer Inc. released a "Flavour Wheel for Maple Products." Suddenly, the words to describe maple syrup jumped from one (maple) to an amazing ninety-one (everything from butter and vanilla to kiwi, black licorice and crushed leaves)!

The flavor wheel took six years and the skills of several teams of sensory evaluation experts and maple product professionals to develop. It includes thirteen flavor families that are broken down into thirty-nine subfamilies and ninety-one distinct flavor characteristics.

OPPOSITE: It's hard to talk with your mouth full of buttery sweet maple taffy.

*The Mapple-tree… yields a Sap,
which has a much pleasanter taste than the
best Limonade or Cherry-water, and makes
the wholesomest drink in the world.*

Baron de Lahontan, *New Voyages to North-America, London, 1703*

The big flavor families are Vanilla, Milky, Empyreumatic (toasted/burnt), Floral, Fruity, Spicy, Foreign deterioration, Foreign environment, Plant herbaceous, Plants-forests-humus-cereals, Plant ligneous, Maple and Confectionery. Flavor family Empyreumatic (toasted/burnt), for example, is broken down into light, medium and strong, and each of those categories has more detailed descriptors, such as golden sugar (one of my personal favorites), chocolate or ground black coffee.

The maple flavor wheel attempts to elevate syrup to the same connoisseur level as wine, cheese and chocolate. But it's not just for flavor snobs. The flavor wheel is an excellent way to evaluate quality from season to season and to help syrup lovers decide which product we like best.

ABOVE: This sunlit bottle of amber-colored syrup promises a fuller flavor than do more delicate, pale gold syrups. RIGHT: Agriculture and Agri-Food Canada / Centre Acer's Flavour Wheel for Maple Products. OPPOSITE: Syrup makers often mark each day by filling a small bottle of syrup to compare their production from day to day.

Maple taffy served sweet and hot at the Warkworth Maple Syrup Festival.

To identify the flavors in syrup, Agriculture and Agri-Food Canada / Centre Acer suggest these four easy steps:

1. Pour a little syrup into a glass and take three quick (and deep) sniffs of the syrup. What was your first impression? Then, take a small sip of the syrup and swirl it around in your mouth just like you've seen the wine connoisseurs in movies do it. Now, here's the hard part — spit it out. Take a minute to concentrate on the flavors you experienced when the syrup was in your mouth and then afterward, too.

2. Try to associate the tastes with something you already know. It might remind you of the aromas of an orange peel, a bag of marshmallows or even a bale of hay!

3. Share your flavor ideas with others, if possible — multiple mouths are better than one when it comes to making sense of these flavors. Now, give the flavor a name (for example, a marshmallow scent might remind you of vanilla).

4. Finally, decide if the taste is mild, medium or strong.

Maple flavor tasting takes concentration and lots of imagination, but most people are up for the job. And don't be too hard on yourself if you swallow the syrup — it's a good excuse to try another mouthful!

Which Grade Is Best?

It's really up to you, your taste buds and how you want to use the syrup. My personal favorite is Light, but I keep a bottle of Medium in the fridge for cooking. The bolder tastes of Medium and Amber withstand the heat of cooking better than the more delicate grades.

Flavor	Also known as
Very delicate	No. 1 Extra Light / Grade A Light Amber / Fancy
Delicate	No. 1 Light Grade A / Medium Amber
Distinct	No. 1 Medium Grade A / Dark Amber
Strong	No. 2 Amber / Grade B / Grade B for reprocessing
Very strong	No. 3 Dark / Commercial

The syrup's grade is determined by the amount of light that passes through it. This grading kit helps Canadian syrup makers know whether their syrup is extra light, dark or somewhere in between.

Is Maple Syrup Good For You?

You bet it is! Maple syrup is a source of iron, potassium, magnesium, calcium and phosphorous. Maple syrup has a higher calcium content than milk! It also contains small amounts of amino acids and proteins, and trace amounts of vitamins B2 (riboflavin), B5 (pantothenic acid) and niacin.

*Good health and
good sense are two
of life's greatest
blessings.*

Syrus (Publilius Syrus), *Maxims*

CALORIE COMPARISON OF POPULAR SWEETENERS	
Sweetener	Calories per Tablespoon
Maple Syrup	40
Molasses	40
Honey	45
Brown Sugar	53
Cane (white) Sugar	55
Corn Syrup	60

If you're looking to count calories, maple syrup is the best way to go. It has fewer calories by volume than white sugar, honey and just about every available natural sweetener.

So how does pure maple syrup compare to those store-bought imitation syrups? Imitation syrups are usually made with corn syrup (more calories) and little to no (zero to two percent) real maple syrup. Try maple syrup anywhere you use sugar. Once you taste the best, you'll forget about the rest.

Cooking with Maple

SEVERAL COOKBOOKS AND WEB SITES PROVIDE SOME UNIVERSAL RULES FOR substituting maple syrup for sugar when cooking and baking. I have discovered these rules are little more than a starting point, because every day brings new conditions to my kitchen. It's a little like trying to find the boiling point of water while making maple syrup. Changes in humidity and temperature can mean that one day the "rule" is perfect; the next, I'm off by a country mile.

In general, there are two things to remember — maple syrup is sweeter than sugar (so cut back on the syrup) and it adds extra moisture (so either cut back on the liquid or increase your dry ingredients a little bit). For every cup (250 mL) of sugar in a recipe, replace it with ¾ cup (175 mL) of maple syrup. (Molasses and honey can be replaced with an equal amount of maple syrup.) This rule doesn't apply to baking. When substituting syrup for sugar in baking, use ¾ cup (175 mL) of syrup for every cup (250 mL) of sugar *and* reduce the main liquid in the recipe by three tablespoons (45 mL). When in doubt, reduce the milk or water in the recipe before you reduce the oil or egg liquid.

OPPOSITE: The youngest Pudifin girl enjoys Maple Marinated Chicken Wings (see recipe, page 88).

Remember, however, that syrup is a lot darker in color than sugar and that the maple color shows in your final product. (Stick to sugar if you need your finished product to be bright white.) Also, maple syrup tends to make your baked goods brown faster than sugar, so watch them carefully as they bake.

Maple syrup is an ingredient you should take very seriously. It can overwhelm every dish it's in if used too heavily or carelessly. It should not be poured liberally over every root vegetable you can find…unless you're looking for a sugar headache and a cavity or two. There's no better way to turn off your family and friends than to submerge their main course in something sweeter than their dessert.

There is no love sincerer than the love of food.

George Bernard Shaw,
Man and Superman

I try to treat maple syrup the way I treat my beloved balsamic vinegar and freshly ground black pepper — all are best if added right at the end of cooking instead of somewhere in the middle. This works wonderfully with most dishes, but doesn't apply to those where syrup is a main ingredient. I've also discovered that maple syrup is utterly fantastic when paired with savory ingredients such as black pepper, chili sauce, curry, soya sauce and, yes, even rhubarb.

For many, though, maple syrup will be forever married to pancakes and nothing more. The thought of slightly warmed syrup cascading over a curl of sweet butter and down the sides of a stack of fluffy, golden pancakes is enough to make anyone's mouth water. How you use your syrup is really up to you. If you'd like to test your syrup cooking mettle, here are a few recipes that are fairly simple and really quite tasty.

Sometimes, pancakes and maple syrup are too good to eat with just a fork.

Maple Caramel Corn

Maple caramel corn is the brainchild of Rachael Bell of Fergus, Ontario. Rachael is a writer and editor who tempts her family, friends and clients with this delicious concoction every holiday season. She rarely reveals her culinary secrets.

Humid weather can play tricks with this recipe, and great care must be taken to ensure the caramel mixture is not overheated (it will quickly become granular).

This recipe can be made without the almonds and pecans, as in the photo at left.

10 heaping cups (2.5 L) plain popped popcorn
1 cup (250 mL) pecan halves
1 cup (250 mL) whole almonds
1 cup (½ lb or 250 mL) butter
½ cup (125 mL) maple syrup
⅔ cup (160 mL) brown sugar
⅔ cup (160 mL) white sugar
1 tsp (5 mL) vanilla
½ tsp (2 mL) baking soda

- Roast nuts in the oven. Combine popcorn and nuts in a large roasting pan, making sure the nuts are evenly distributed.

- In a medium-size saucepan, blend the butter, sugars and maple syrup over medium-high heat, stirring until completely melted. Insert a candy thermometer. Do not stir mixture after this point. Cook the caramel mixture until it reaches 280°F (140°C). Remove the caramel from the heat, add vanilla and baking soda and stir rapidly making sure the soda is well blended. Immediately pour the caramel over the popcorn.

- With a large wooden spoon or spatula, quickly stir the caramel and popcorn until the corn is completely covered. Don't let the caramel touch your hands: it is very hot! Transfer the popcorn onto two baking sheets. Gingerly pat it down until it is flat on the baking sheets.

- To quickly cool the candy, place the baking sheets in the refrigerator. When cool, the candy should easily break into bite-size pieces. Store your candy in an airtight container.

Sucrerie de la Montagne's World-Famous Maple Sugar Pie

Sucrerie de la Montagne's owner Pierre Faucher serves this delicious dessert as part of the traditional Quebecois-style sugaring-off meals served at his award-winning sugar house in Rigaud, Quebec. The recipe is a family tradition, passed down from his mother to him, and now to you.

*Maple sugar can be found in specialty stores and some health food stores. Brown sugar can be substituted if maple sugar is not available.

2 cups (500 mL) milk
2 egg yolks, beaten
¾ cup (180 mL) maple sugar*, packed
½ cup (125 mL) flour
½ tsp (2 mL) salt
1 tbsp (15 mL) butter

- Heat milk in the top of a double boiler (be careful not to scald the milk). When hot, take a little milk and beat into egg yolks. Add beaten yolks to hot milk.

- In a separate bowl, mix together maple sugar and flour. Whisk mixture gradually into hot milk. Remove from heat and add salt and butter. Allow to cool.

- Pour mixture into a baked pie crust. (Make your own or, for quick results, use a pre-made crust available in the freezer section of the grocery store.) Chill. Cut into slices and serve with a dollop of whipped cream.

Variation: Try adding ¼ tsp or so of ground black pepper. I know it sounds strange to add something savory to something sweet, but it really gives the pie a satisfying bite.

See www.sucreriedelamontagne.com

Maple Sugar Pecans

Megan Loppe of Toronto, Ontario, created this recipe to satisfy her maple-loving partner, who would add maple syrup to everything if she let him! Megan, the daughter of my dear friend Jane, is constantly experimenting with new syrup combinations and has perfected the delicate art of using maple syrup as a subtle spice instead of an overwhelming sweet.

2 generous cups (500 mL) pecan halves
⅓ cup (80 mL) maple syrup
Sprinkle bourbon or rye (optional)
Pinch salt

- Preheat your oven to 350°F (175°C). Line a baking sheet with foil. (This makes cleanup a lot easier!) Spread pecans evenly on cookie sheet and drizzle with maple syrup (and whiskey, if you're using it). Sprinkle with salt to taste and toss.

- Bake, stirring occasionally, until syrup coats pecans and pecans are toasted, about 7 to 10 minutes. Allow to cool (the syrup will crystallize as the nuts cool). Store in airtight container and eat quickly… before your family finds them!

Variation: For the adventurous only — replace the whiskey with ¼ tsp of cayenne pepper or chili powder, or both, depending on your heat tolerance. There's nothing quite like a sweet heat.

Taft's Apple Pancake

Mary Taft of Taft's Milk and Maple Farm in Huntington, Vermont, created this deliciously easy twist on a traditional favorite. Mary, Bruce and son Tim not only run a 5,000-tap maple operation, they also manage a large dairy enterprise with 150 head of beautiful registered Jersey cows.

2 large cooking apples, sliced as for pie

1 tsp. (5 mL) cinnamon

¼ cup (60 mL) butter, melted

¼ cup (60 mL) chopped pecans

⅓ cup (80 mL) maple or brown sugar

Your favorite pancake batter

- Preheat your oven to 450°F (230°C). In a 9- to 10-inch ovenproof skillet, sauté sliced apples in butter over medium heat until tender. Remove skillet from heat and add nuts. Pour prepared pancake batter over apples and sprinkle with sugar and cinnamon. Bake 15 minutes until puffy and sugar is melted. Use a pie plate if an oven-proof skillet is not available. Smother with pure maple syrup and enjoy!

See www.vtmaplesyrup.com

Maple Dressing

Desperation sometimes leads to creativity in my house, particularly when the salad dressing bottle is empty. This time, the experiment worked!

6 parts canola oil (olive oil works, too)

2 parts apple cider or balsamic vinegar

2 parts maple syrup

1 part Dijon mustard

Freshly ground black pepper to taste

- Whisk together, pour over your salad and enjoy!

Maple Marinated Chicken Wings

This delicious recipe was created by Kathy Desmarais of Black Sheep Sugarhouse of Orleans, Vermont. Kathy, her husband, Rene, and their son Andre have approximately 10,000 taps on 600 acres nestled in Vermont's fabled Green Mountains. The land now owned by the Desmarais family once belonged to Ira Allen, brother of famed Revolutionary War hero Ethan Allen.

3 lbs (1.4 kg) chicken wings
¾ cup (180 mL) soya sauce
1½ tsp (8 mL) ground ginger
1 tsp (5 mL) ground mustard
¼ tsp (1 mL) garlic powder
(add more if you love garlic)
1½ tbsp (22 mL) maple syrup
1 tsp (5 mL) dried chives

- Cut tips off chicken wings and pierce each wing with a fork. Mix remaining ingredients in a separate bowl; reserve some sauce for basting wings during cooking. Place a layer of wings in a bowl or baking pan. Pour enough marinade over wings to coat them. Continue to add layers of wings and marinade, one layer at a time, until all of the sauce is used.

- Cover and refrigerate for at least 4 hours. Remove from refrigerator.

- Preheat oven to 375°F (190°C). Arrange wings on foil-covered baking sheet. Use a pastry brush to paint each wing with a dab of the reserved sauce. Bake for 45 to 55 minutes.

Variation: For those of you who watch your salt intake, substitute reduced-salt soya sauce for the regular version.

See www.blacksheepsugarhouse.com

Maple Salmon

Sue Edwards, who owns and operates the Country Caterer in Orangeville, Ontario (519-940-8460),
is often asked to prepare this delicious dish for the many events she caters. Sue's spontaneous nature is mirrored in the recipe — the ingredients are added in amounts you feel are appropriate rather than in a restrictive list. Maple salmon has made me a star with dinner guests more than once!

1 long filet of salmon
1 clove of garlic, minced
Olive oil
Maple syrup
Fresh, cracked black pepper

- Preheat the oven to 450°F (230°C). Wash the salmon and place it, skin side down, in a shallow baking or roasting pan. Drizzle the salmon with olive oil and rub it into the flesh. Next, rub the garlic into the flesh. Grind black pepper over the fish and rub it in, too. Finally, drizzle the salmon with maple syrup and rub it into the flesh.

- Bake in the center of the oven for 14 minutes.

Variation: Maple salmon can also be barbecued over medium-high heat. Small pieces of salmon can also be used, but the cooking time must be shortened.

Grandma Pym's
Maple Nut Crème Pudding

My maternal grandmother, Olive Pym, made this recipe for special occasions only. Feeding hearty and healthy meals to six young mouths (plus Grandpa) through the hardships of the lean years took priority over "fancy" dishes like this.

2 cups (500 mL) milk

1 cup (250 mL) maple syrup

2 eggs

2 tbsp (30 mL) corn starch

Pinch salt

1 cup (250 mL) chopped pecans

1 cup (250 mL) cream

- Heat 1¾ cups (430 mL) milk and maple syrup in double boiler. Combine remaining milk with corn starch and salt. Add to hot mixture, stirring constantly. Cook for approximately two minutes.

- Take a little of the milk mixture and beat into eggs. Add eggs to mixture in double boiler and cook for four minutes.

- Pour into individual dishes and sprinkle with nuts. Eat hot or put in fridge to set and serve cold.

Variation: The original recipe called for walnuts but I prefer pecans. Use walnuts if you like them better.

Acknowledgments

The book would not have been possible without the support, in one form or another, of several wonderful people and organizations:
Kathy Desmarais, Black Sheep Sugarhouse, Orleans, Vermont; Mary Taft, Taft's Milk and Maple Farm, Huntington, Vermont; Jacques and Pauline Couture, Couture's Maple Shop & Bed and Breakfast, Westfield, Vermont; Ken and Rene McCutcheon, McCutcheon's Maple Syrup, Coldwater, Ontario; Leek Farms, Alliston, Ontario; Lorraine O'Byrne, Black Creek Pioneer Village, Toronto, Ontario; Nelson Carter; Jane and Megan Loppe; Dorothy Fetterly; Rosemary Molesworth; Steve Brown, Dufferin County Museum and Archives; Kortright Centre for Conservation, Kleinburg, Ontario; Bruce's Mill Conservation Area, Stouffville, Ontario; Crawford Lake Conservation Area, Campbellville, Ontario; Sandy Flats Sugar Bush and Pancake House, Warkworth, Ontario; Warkworth Maple Syrup Festival; Elmira Maple Syrup Festival; and last (but definitely not least), coon-capped Bob Finney from Bob's Sugar Shack, Caledon East, Ontario.

Special thanks is extended the following individuals whose generosity and assistance went well beyond any regular call of duty. Without these folks, this book would only be a shell of what you see and read today:
Pierre Faucher, Sucrerie de la Montage, Riguad, Quebec (thank you for making us feel like we were part of your family); John Williams and Carl Kampitelli, Pine House Farm, Hillsdale, Ontario; Dick and Gale O'Brien, Uncle Richard's Maple Syrup and Supplies, Priceville, Ontario; Lori Cox-Paul, U.S. National Archives and Records Administration (NARA), Central Plains Region; Michèle LaRose, Agriculture and Agri-Food Canada; Kathleen Fraser, Noel Hudson and John Denison, the Boston Mills Press; Andrew Smith, Joseph Gisini, Kevin Cockburn and Daniella Zanchetta, PageWave Graphics; Rachael Bell; Sue Edwards, The Country Caterer, Orangeville, Ontario; Rick and Diane Marsh, Vermont Maple Outlet, Jeffersonville, Vermont; Albert Martin, Ontario Maple Syrup Museum, St. Jacobs, Ontario; Russell and Pam Stewart, Rosemont General Store, Rosemont, Ontario; and Sally and Jefferson Mappin.

From the photographer:
Thank you to Janet, my partner in yet another collaboration,
for all her hard work in putting her wonderfully engaging text to paper.

From the writer:
Thank you to Rose for once again capturing the heart of this topic —
her photos make my words leap from the paper.

Selected Sources

"Address of Thanksgiving to the Powers of the Master of Life (Green Corn Dance)," *Seneca Fiction, Legends and Myths (Part 2)*, collected and translated by J.N.B. Hewitt in 1896 on the Cattaraugus Reservation, N.Y. Thirty-second Annual Report on the Bureau of American Ethnology to the Secretary of Smithsonian Institution, 1910–1911 (1918).

Agriculture and Agri-Food Canada / Centre Acer Inc. *Flavour Wheel for Maple Products.* Available at www.agr.gc.ca/roue_erable/.

Agriculture and Agri-Food Canada. *Canadian Maple Products Situations and Trends 2006-2007.*

Baron de Lahontan. *New Voyages to North-America.* London: 1703. The Tracy W. McGregor Library of American History.

Chapeskie, Dave. *The Maple Syrup Industry in Ontario — Answers to Commonly Asked Questions and References.* Ontario Ministry of Agriculture, Food and Rural Affairs, March 1997.

Davenport, Anni L. and Lewis J. Staats. *Maple Syrup Production for the Beginner.* School of Forest Resources, Pennsylvania State University, and Department of Natural Resources, Cornell University, Cornell Cooperative Extension, 1998.

Heilingmann, R.B. and M.R. Koelling, eds. *North American Maple Syrup Producers Manual.* Ohio State University Extension, 1996.

Holland, J.G. [1819–1881, publisher unknown]

Jefferson, Thomas. *To M. Lasteyrie.* Washington: Washington ed. v. 314, July 1808.

Langenberg, W.J. and J.W. Butler. *Maple Syrup: Measuring Density (Fact Sheet).* Ontario Ministry of Agriculture and Food, May 1989.

Lawrence, James M., Rux Martin, and Paul Boisvert. *Sweet Maple.* Vermont: Chapters Publishing Ltd. and Vermont Life Magazine, 1993.

Muir, A. "The Maple Leaf Forever." Toronto: "published for the author," and printed at the Guardian Office, publishing outlet for the Methodist Book Room, 1867.

Nearing, Helen and Scott. *The Maple Sugar Book.* New York: Schocken Books, 1972.

Ontario Maple Syrup Producers Association. "Maple Production Survey Results 2005." Available at www.ontariomaple.com/research/

Ontario Ministry of Natural Resources. *Backyard Maple Syrup Production — Extension Notes.* Landowner Resource Centre and the Ontario Ministry of Natural Resources, 1995.

Parr Strickland Trail, C. *The Canadian Settler's Guide.* London, E. Stanford, 1860.

Publius Syrus, 42 B.C. Maxim 827.

Sangster, M.E. "Awakening." [1838–1912, publisher unknown].

Shaw, G.B. "Man and Superman." 1903. Available as Project Gutenberg e-Book at www.gutenberg.org/etext/3328.

Vermont Maple Sugar Maker's Association. "2011 Vermont Maple Syrup Production Figures — Vermont led all States in production with 1,140,000 gallons, an increase of 28 percent from 2010 and the highest on record in over sixty years." Available at www.vermontmaple.org

Waugh, F. M. *Iroquois Foods and Food Preparation.* Ottawa Govt. Printing Bureau, 1916

Wells, K.M. *The Owl Pen.* Garden City, N.Y: Doubleday, 1969

Photo Credits

All photographs by Rosemary Hasner except as otherwise noted.

Page 10: Photograph No. NRE-75-RL(PHO)-1068 (ARC285761); "Maple Sugar Industry, 1939," 1939; Department of the Interior. Bureau of Indian Affairs. Red Lake Agency. Record Group 75: Records of the Bureau of Indian Affairs, 1793–1989; Series: Red Lake Agency: Photographs, 1910–1965; National Archives and Records Administration — Central Plains Region (Kansas City).

Page 13: Photograph No. NRE-75-RL(PHO)-1072 (ARC285760); "Maple Sugar Industry, 1939," 1939; Department of the Interior. Bureau of Indian Affairs. Red Lake Agency. Record Group 75: Records of the Bureau of Indian Affairs, 1793–1989; Series: Red Lake

Agency: Photographs, 1910–1965; National Archives and Records Administration — Central Plains Region (Kansas City).

Page 16: Men emptying maple sap buckets, ca. 1925, Archives of Ontario, RG-2-71, YZ-11. I0004354.

Page 18: Pioneers boiling sap outdoors in Ontario, ca. 1910, Photographer: John Boyd, Library and Archives Canada, RD-000054.

Page 43: Man tapping a maple tree for sap, ca. 1925, Archives of Ontario, RG-2-71, YZ-5. I0004353.

Images pages 9, 20, 23 (all): The Henderson family of Millbank, Ontario, circa 1920. Access to images courtesy of the Maple Syrup Museum of Ontario; rephotographed by Rosemary Hasner.

Index